FIRST REPERTOIRE
for LITTLE PIANISTS

BOOK 1

by Melanie Spanswick

Cover illustration by Laura Benavente

ISBN: 978-1-70515-472-4

EXCLUSIVELY DISTRIBUTED BY

Copyright © 2022 by The Willis Music Co.
International Copyright Secured All Rights Reserved

Visit Hal Leonard Online at
www.halleonard.com

Contact us:
Hal Leonard
7777 West Bluemound Road
Milwaukee, WI 53213
Email: info@halleonard.com

In Europe, contact:
Hal Leonard Europe Limited
42 Wigmore Street
Marylebone, London, W1U 2RY
Email: info@halleonardeurope.com

In Australia, contact:
Hal Leonard Australia Pty. Ltd.
4 Lentara Court
Cheltenham, Victoria, 3192 Australia
Email: info@halleonard.com.au

PREFACE

ORIGINAL REPERTOIRE

First Repertoire for Little Pianists is a repertoire series for children from beginner to early elementary level. Each book contains a collection of 25 original piano pieces, including a selection of solo works (some with teacher accompaniment) and concert duets to be played with either a teacher or fellow student.

BOOK 1

"Book 1" consists of very short compositions up to 17 measures in length, which may be used alongside various piano method books or as performance pieces. The journey begins using separate hands, gradually combining both hands together.

FIVE-FINGER HAND POSITIONS

Focusing mainly on simplistic, five-finger hand positions, "Book 1" features a useful keyboard diagram at the top of each piece, indicating note positions. Accompanying performance notes are included alongside each piece. These are intended to help facilitate interpretation, note learning, and rhythmic literacy.

NOTE AND RHYTHMIC LEARNING

Understanding of rhythm is fundamental in the early stages of musical learning. This book focuses on whole, dotted half, half, and quarter-note time values, and employs the following time signatures: 2/4, 3/4, and 4/4. Key signatures are limited to C major/A minor, G major, and F major, with the addition of some pentatonic pieces.

DEVELOPING MUSICIANSHIP

Dynamics, phrase markings, tempo markings, fingering, and pedaling (where appropriate) are present throughout. There is also a selection of rote pieces along the way, to encourage movement around the keyboard.

HAVING FUN

There are also fun illustrations interspersed throughout this book, designed to fuel the imagination. Coloring these in will be an engaging activity, helping to facilitate further investment in the learning process.

Melanie Spanswick

CONTENTS

ALOHA

SOLO WITH TEACHER ACCOMPANIMENT

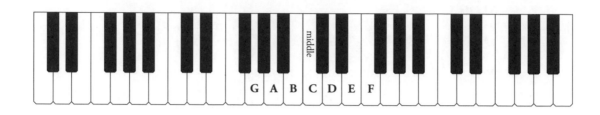

Sprightly

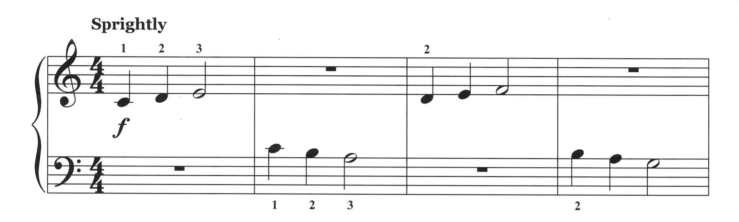

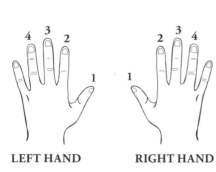

LEFT HAND   **RIGHT HAND**

ACCOMPANIMENT

Sprightly

PERFORMANCE NOTES

In Hawaii, people use the word "aloha" as a greeting. Welcome to *First Repertoire for Little Pianists* and your early stages of piano discovery.

RHYTHM FOCUS

Rhythm refers to the patterns of long and short notes in music. Have a go at tapping out the rhythm of the piece. It has four counts per bar. Try to tap your right hand on the piano lid or your knee as if you are a ticking clock: steady and regular. Now do it again and count "1, 2, 3, 4" as you tap.

To tap the rhythm of "Aloha," you'll need both hands. Be sure to use the right hand to tap the note values in the treble clef and the left hand for those in the bass clef. Here, the crossed noteheads show that there is no pitch.

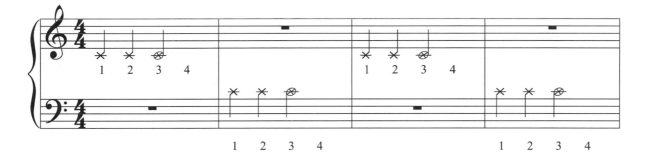

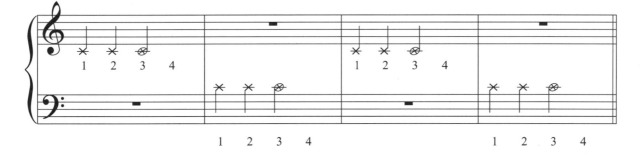

NOTE FOCUS

When we are learning to read notes, it can help to write them out. Find the different notes used in this piece and write them out once on the grand staff below. Write each note as a notehead without a stem. Once you've done this, write the letter names underneath. The first one has been done for you.

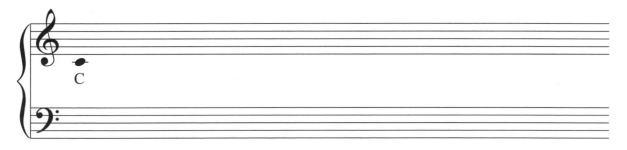

5

SMOOTH 'N' SPIKY

SOLO WITH TEACHER ACCOMPANIMENT

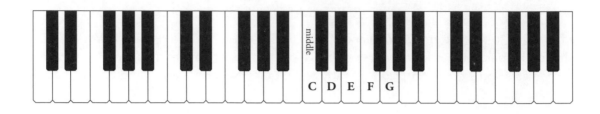

Moderato

RIGHT HAND

ACCOMPANIMENT

PERFORMANCE NOTES

Can you think of everyday objects that are smooth and spiky? Keep these in mind when playing the music!

RHYTHM FOCUS

Tap out the rhythm with your right hand. Keep a very steady pulse and say the beat count as you tap. The 𝄽 shows a quarter rest. This symbol means silence for one count. Try sniffing or clapping in the rests.

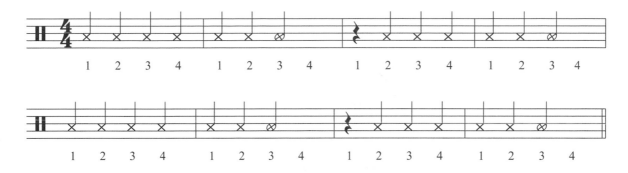

NOTE FOCUS

Here is an extract from the piece. Try saying the letter names to the correct rhythm. Then, try singing them, using the letter names as the lyrics. The letter names are in the noteheads.

This piece features two different types of finger touch (or *articulation*).

Noteheads that are grouped by a curved line must be smoothly joined together. Make sure your fingers move from note to note without any sound "gaps" in between. This articulation is known as *legato*.

Noteheads that have dots underneath must be crisp, short, and detached. To jump off each note quickly, try to imagine that the key is red hot! This articulation is known as *staccato*.

MERRY-GO-ROUND

SOLO WITH TEACHER ACCOMPANIMENT

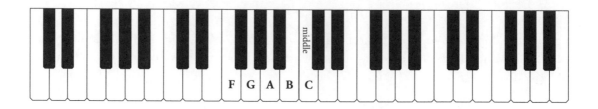

This note needs a deeper touch

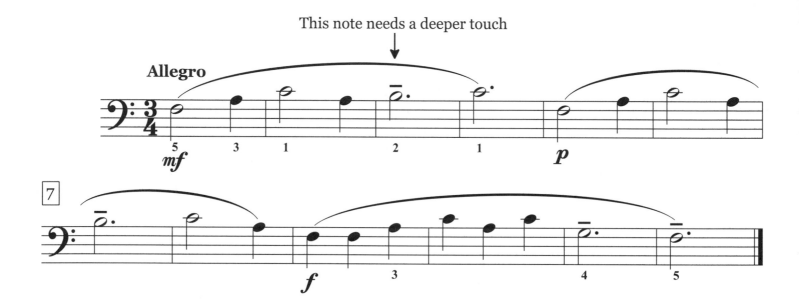

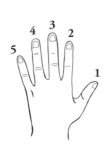

LEFT HAND

ACCOMPANIMENT

PERFORMANCE NOTES

This piece is for your left hand only. Your teacher will play the accompaniment and together you will both sound wonderful. Imagine riding happily on a merry-go-round as the music plays.

RHYTHM FOCUS

Have a go at tapping the rhythm on your piano lid (or your knee), using your left hand. Say the beat count, too. Here, we have three quarter-note beats per bar, so you'll be counting "1, 2, 3."

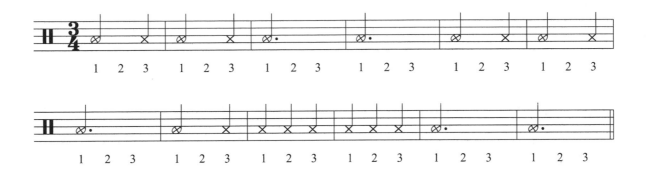

NOTE FOCUS

Can you write the bass-clef sign? After you have drawn it a few times on the staffs below, write and name the first and last note of the piece.

SUNSET

SOLO

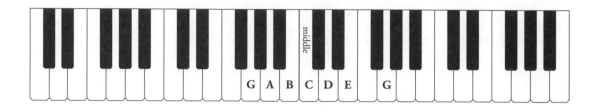

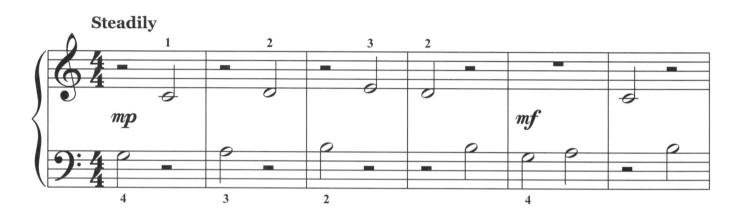

LEFT HAND   RIGHT HAND

PERFORMANCE NOTES

The sun warms the evening sky with an orange glow as it sets. Try drawing a sunset and keeping this image in mind as you play this piece steadily and smoothly.

RHYTHM FOCUS

To tap the rhythm of "Sunset," you'll need both hands. Be sure to use the right hand to tap the note values in the treble clef and the left hand for those in the bass clef.

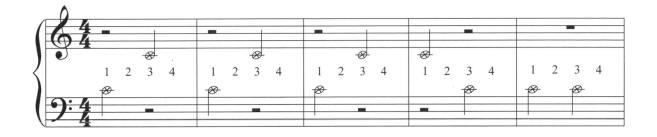

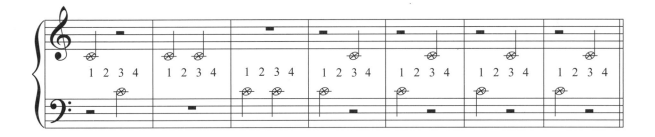

NOTE FOCUS

This is your first solo piano piece. It uses both hands but they don't play at the same time. You'll need to play four notes with your left hand (G, A, B, and C) and four notes with your right hand (C, D, E, and G). Can you find the notes in each hand on the keyboard for the notation below?

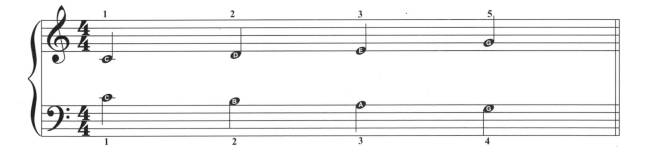

The dynamics have been written into the score. Once you have played them, have a go at adding your own.

WALKING ON STILTS

SOLO WITH TEACHER ACCOMPANIMENT

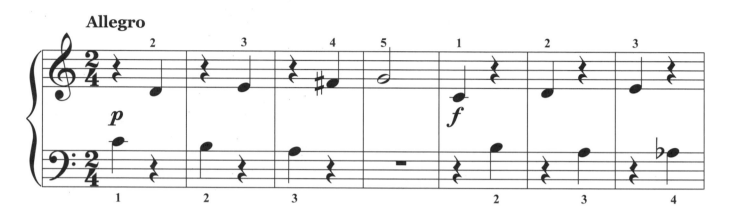

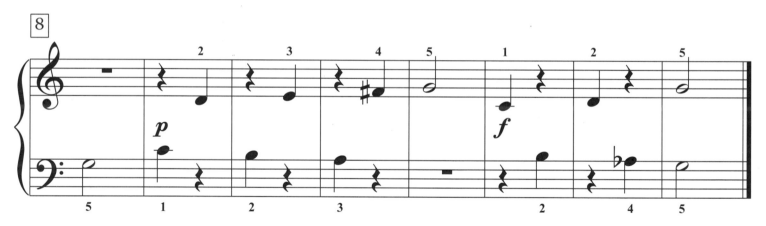

ACCOMPANIMENT

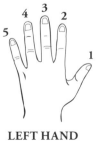
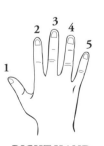

LEFT HAND   **RIGHT HAND**

PERFORMANCE NOTES

"Walking on Stilts" is a bit like walking up and down steps: piano steps. In the first four measures, each note moves outwards away from middle C. The left-hand part moves "down" the keyboard and the right-hand part moves "up." When both hands move in opposite directions like this, we say they are moving in *contrary motion*.

RHYTHM FOCUS

Tap the rhythm on your knee or piano lid. When we say the beat count, we will count "1, 2." This is because there are two quarter-note beats per bar.

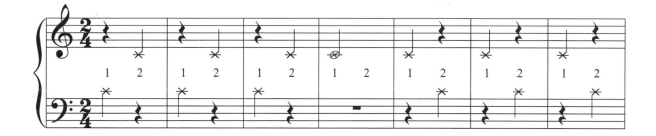

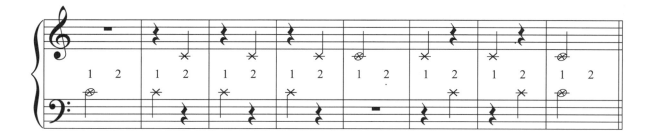

NOTE FOCUS

Have a look at the keyboard diagram above the music. For this piece, we are playing two black keys, F♯ and A♭. See if you can find the notes on the music and circle them.

When we see a ♯, it means we must play the black key immediately to the right of that note.

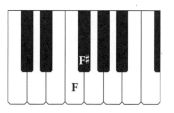

When we see a ♭, it means we must play the black key immediately to the left of that note.

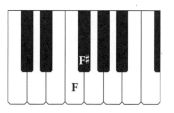

As black keys are smaller and narrower than white keys, our fingers need to be ready to play. Be sure to move the relevant finger forward in plenty of time, hovering over the black key.

SECRET JOURNEY

SOLO

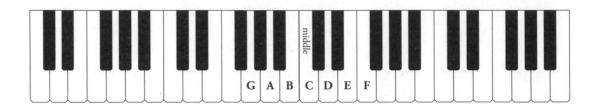

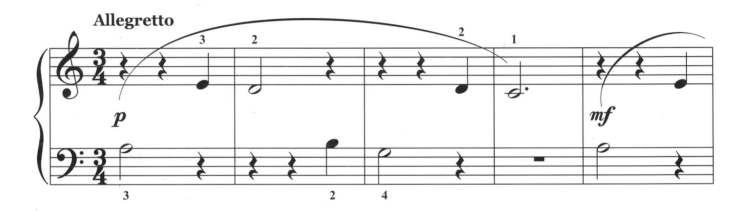

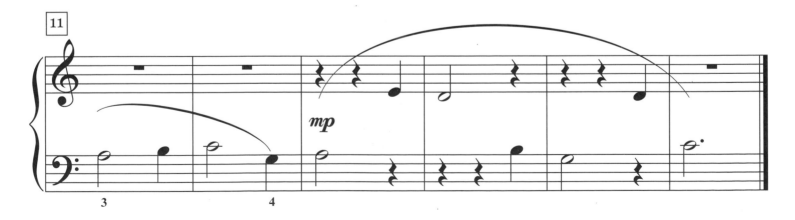

PERFORMANCE NOTES

There's something very exciting about a secret journey. It's rather like starting a new piece of music. What will you discover? What will you learn? Enjoy the joy of getting to know music for the first time.

RHYTHM FOCUS

To tap the rhythm of "Secret Journey," you'll need both hands. Be sure to use the right hand to tap the note values in the treble clef and the left hand for those in the bass clef. Say the beat count as you tap. Remember, you are going to count "1, 2, 3" because there are three quarter-note beats per bar.

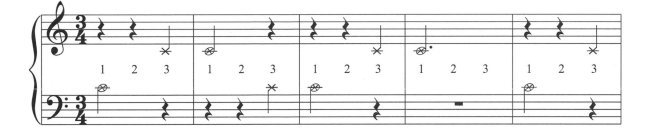

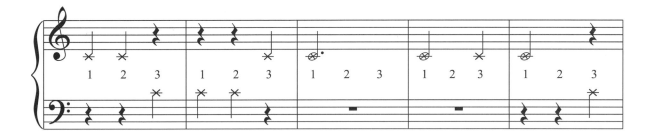

NOTE FOCUS

Find the notes used in this piece and write them out on the grand staff below. Write each note as a notehead without a stem. Once you've written the notes out, write the letter names underneath. The first one has been done for you.

A

15

STROLLING

SOLO WITH TEACHER ACCOMPANIMENT

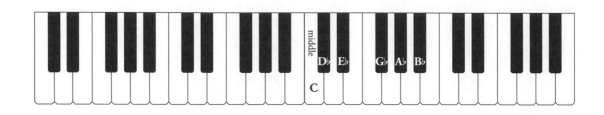

LEFT HAND   **RIGHT HAND**

ACCOMPANIMENT

PERFORMANCE NOTES

When we stroll, we walk at a relaxed, steady pace. This should be the pace at which you try to perform this music.

RHYTHM FOCUS

Let's play tic-tac-toe! Ask your teacher to play with you using quarter notes (the 0s), and you can play using half notes (the Xs). Place the half notes in a row of three before your teacher places their quarter notes and you have won the game! To help, a half note has already been added.

NOTE FOCUS

This piece uses only black keys. You'll learn the music by rote, memorizing the note patterns. Your teacher will tell you which notes to play. You will learn where the notes sit on the keyboard without needing to read the music, so you'll know the piece by heart.

Both hands play in the treble clef for this piece. Can you draw a treble clef? Have a go at writing a few on the staff below.

BEDTIME STORY

SOLO WITH TEACHER ACCOMPANIMENT

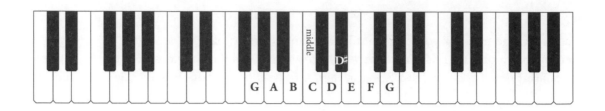

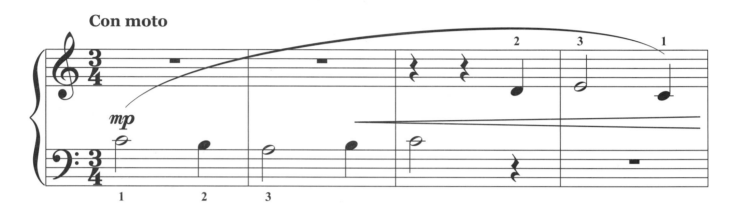

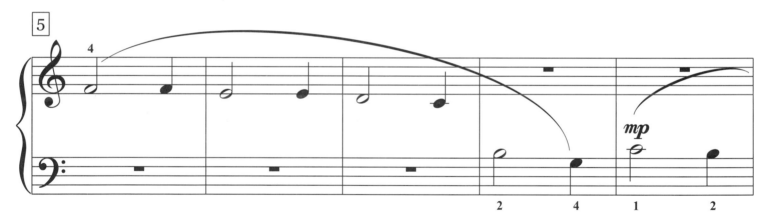

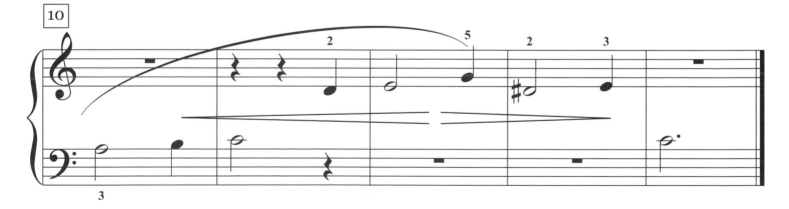

PERFORMANCE NOTES

We all love a good bedtime story to make us feel warm, safe, and loved. Play this music as if it's the last thing you are going to hear before a good night's sleep.

RHYTHM FOCUS

Try to put greater emphasis on the first beat of each measure and less on the third beat. (The weight of your finger on the keys should be greater on beat 1 than on beat 3.) This will help to make your performance extra special.

NOTE FOCUS

The melody is split between your right hand and left hand. Both hands must create a bold, full sound throughout the piece. (The notes in the right hand should not be noticeably louder than those in the left hand.) Make sure that you can be clearly heard above your teacher's accompaniment part.

Write out the notes in this piece as noteheads without a stem. Then, write the correct letter name underneath each note. Watch out for the D♯, which you can find using the keyboard diagram.

ACCOMPANIMENT

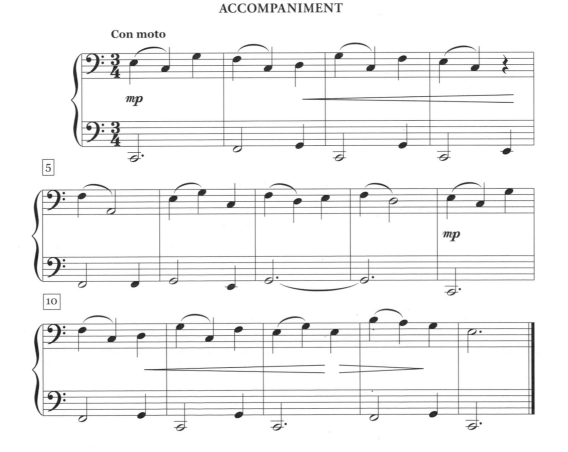

19

STICKY FINGERS

DUET

PERFORMANCE NOTES

Music is enjoyed best with friends. This duet is intended for you to play with a fellow student. Enjoy exploring music as a team and having fun with this piece, perhaps even making up your own dynamics together.

RHYTHM FOCUS

When performing duets, it is so important that you play perfectly in time with one another. Practice this by tapping the simple rhythm below, saying the beat count together. Try sniffing or clapping in the rests!

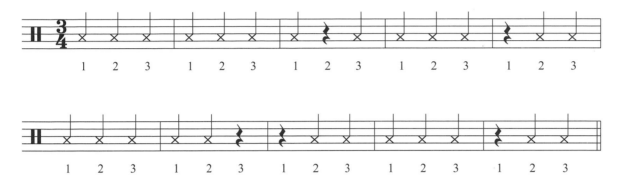

NOTE FOCUS

This piece is made from a scale with only five notes. Find and name the five notes that you play. A scale containing only five notes is called a *pentatonic scale*.

To play an excellent duet, both players must be completely together. Do your best to ensure that every note in both parts sounds at exactly the same moment. Why not record yourselves playing the piece on a phone or other device? Listen back and see how together your playing is.

A note for "Player 1." You will see that your music has this symbol above the staff: *8ᵛᵃ* - - - - - - -. This means that you need to play the notes an octave higher than written.

ANGEL'S DELIGHT

SOLO WITH TEACHER ACCOMPANIMENT

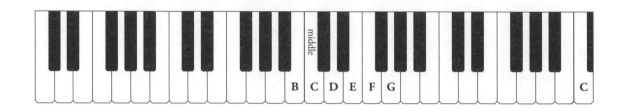

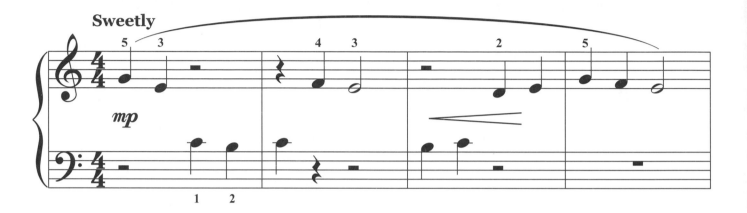

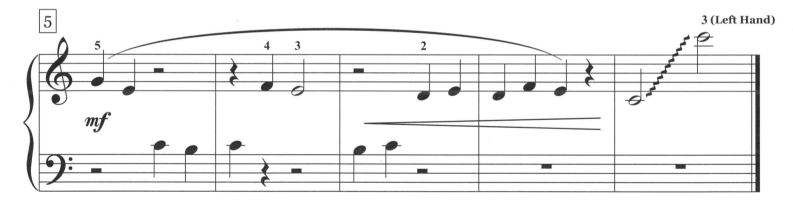

ACCOMPANIMENT

PERFORMANCE NOTES

Practice this piece thoroughly and enjoy making the music sound truly angelic.

NOTE FOCUS

Be sure to sound like a beautiful angel by seeing how softly you can play during the first two measures. A sweet tone will bring your angel to life; aim to use a smooth (*legato*) touch and avoid any gaps in the sound.

The wavy line between the notes at measure 9 indicates a *glissando*, which means a "slide." Turn your right hand so that the palm is facing upwards. Then, place the back of your fingers (balancing on your fingernails) over the notes.

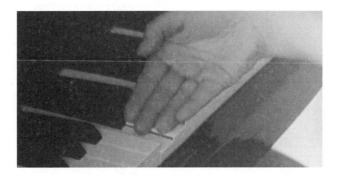

You will need to depress the white keys from middle C to the C two octaves higher. To do this, slide across each note with the back of your fingers (it's more comfortable to rest on the fingernails). Land firmly on the top C, which can be played by the third finger of your left hand. If you do this at speed, the effect will be similar to that of an angel rising up into the clouds.

Practice your glissando using the following note patterns.

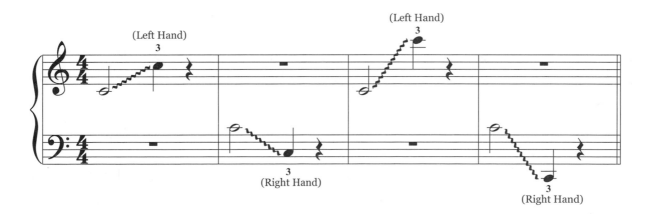

FLYING HIGH

SOLO WITH TEACHER ACCOMPANIMENT

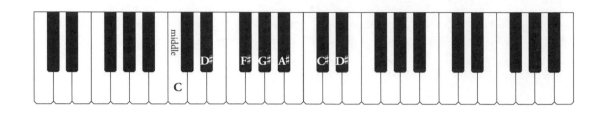

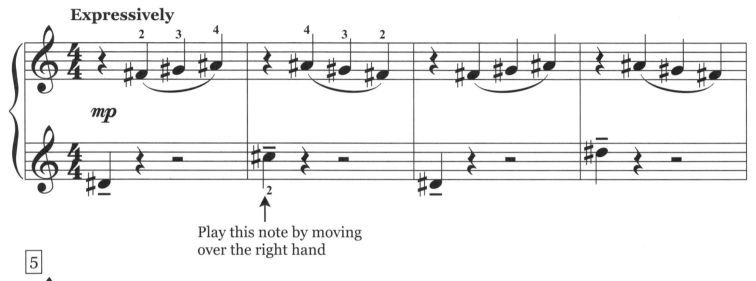

Play this note by moving
over the right hand

ACCOMPANIMENT

PERFORMANCE NOTES

Birds are so graceful when they are flying high. The world below can also look peaceful when you look out the window of an airplane. Keep this sense of peace and calm when you play this music.

RHYTHM FOCUS

Begin by establishing a steady beat. Say the beat count "1, 2, 3, 4" and tap along. Your beat count and taps should be regular, like that of a heartbeat or the ticking of a clock.

Now, tap the following pattern and say the beat count.

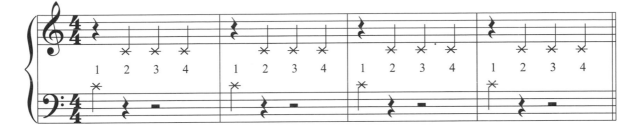

NOTE FOCUS

"Flying High" uses black keys only. It helps if the tips of your fingers are placed firmly in the center of each key for good finger-key connection.

The left-hand part moves over the right hand in measures 2, 4, 6, and 8. Take a look at the piano keyboard above the music and you'll see which notes you need to play.

Move smoothly from note to note in the right-hand part; your wrists and arms should feel relaxed as you play.

MOUSE TRAP

SOLO WITH TEACHER ACCOMPANIMENT

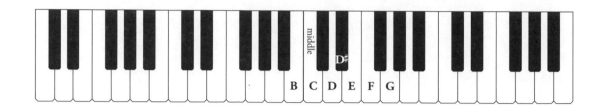

ACCOMPANIMENT

PERFORMANCE NOTES

The little mouse scampers around and he doesn't want to get caught! Keep this image in mind when playing this piece.

NOTE FOCUS

Quarter notes with a dot under or above the notehead must be played with a *staccato* touch. This means the notes should be very short and detached, like a scampering mouse. Try to create a "knocking" effect with each finger, leaving the keys as quickly as possible. Keep the half notes *legato* (smooth).

Watch out for the D♯ in measure 5. The mouse loses his way for just a moment, before scampering back to the melody and arriving safely home. The ♮ in measure 6 means that you return to playing the white D key.

Write out all of the different notes in this piece as noteheads without a stem. Then, write the correct letter name underneath each note.

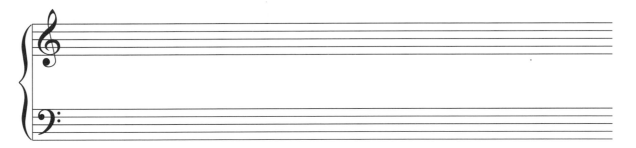

HIDE AND SEEK

SOLO WITH TEACHER ACCOMPANIMENT

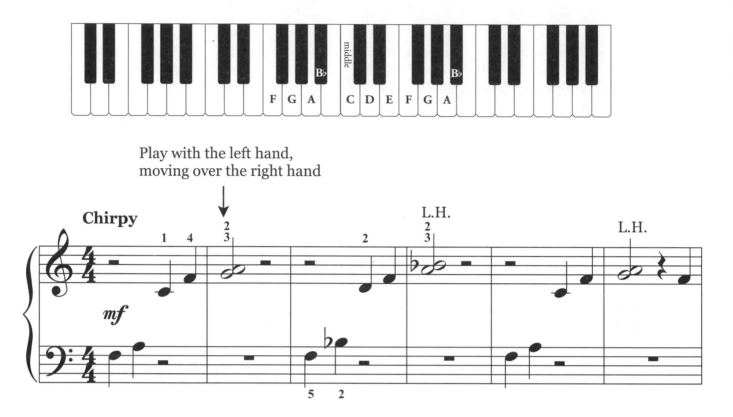

Play with the left hand,
moving over the right hand

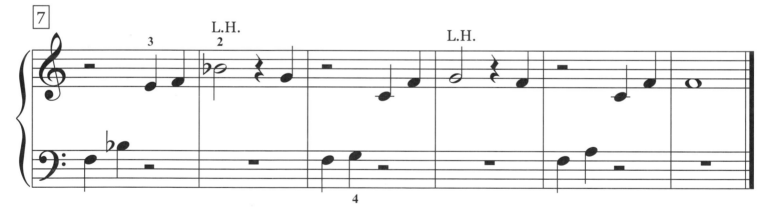

ACCOMPANIMENT

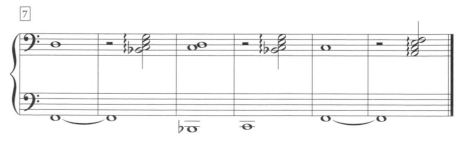

PERFORMANCE NOTES

A game of hide and seek can be such fun with your family or friends. There aren't many dynamics written into the music. Once you are confident with the notes and rhythm, try adding your own to make your performance as interesting as possible.

RHYTHM FOCUS

Look at this four-measure rhythm. Ask your teacher to clap it to you. Then, echo it back by tapping on the piano lid. Both of you should say the beat count, too ("1, 2, 3, 4").

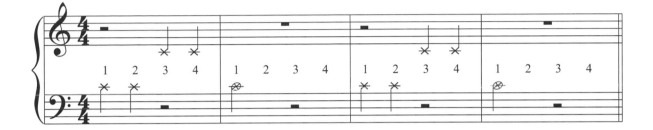

NOTE FOCUS

There is only one dynamic marking in this piece, right at the beginning. You need to add your own to the rest of the music. Will you end softly or loudly? Enjoy experimenting with the sound of the piano and playing the piece in lots of different ways.

In this piece, the left-hand part moves over the right hand in measures 2, 4, 6, 8, and 10. Every half note is played by the left hand. In measures 2, 4, and 6, you will play two notes at the same time. This is called a *dyad*. Enjoy this sound!

Be mindful of the B♭ in measures 3, 4, 7, and 8; place your fingers firmly on the black key to avoid slipping off.

WALTZING FROGS

SOLO WITH TEACHER ACCOMPANIMENT

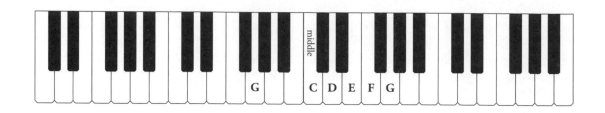

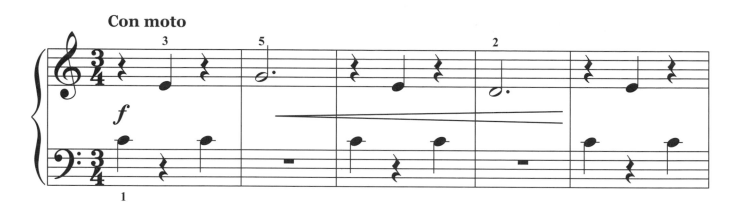

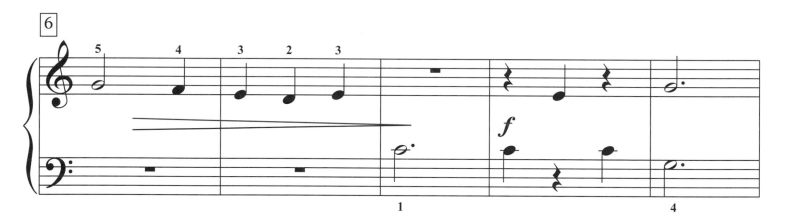

PERFORMANCE NOTES

We all enjoy dancing! A waltz is a ballroom dance undertaken by two people (or in this case, two frogs) who elegantly "glide" (or hop) around the dance floor.

RHYTHM FOCUS

The numbers written at the beginning of the piece (3/4) mean that you need to count three quarter-note beats per bar. This is what gives the waltz its lilting character.

This piece uses the dotted half note. Writing a dot next to a notehead adds half the value of the note it follows. You should count "1, 2, 3" for a dotted half note.

2   +   1   =   3 Beats

NOTE FOCUS

Keep a lovely, smooth *legato* touch throughout, joining every note carefully as the melody moves between your two hands. "Con moto" means "with movement." If the dance is too slow, those frogs are going to fall off their lily pads!

ACCOMPANIMENT

BANG ON THE BEAT

SOLO

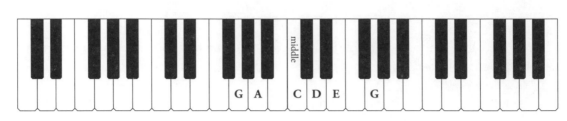

Allegro

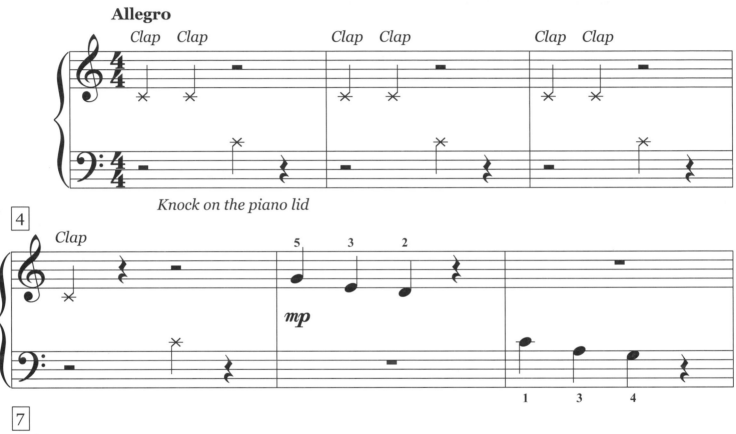

Knock on the piano lid

Knock on the piano lid

PERFORMANCE NOTES

Accurate counting is important when performing music. Here, you are actually going to bang on the beat, so make sure that you pay attention to your counting!

RHYTHM FOCUS

In music, a rest symbol indicates a moment of silence. There are quite a lot of rests in your part. Look out for the quarter-rest symbol: ♩. This shows one beat of silence. Circle all the quarter rests in your solo part. You might like to sniff or clap in these rests when you are practicing the music to make sure you count them correctly.

Try tapping this exercise, which is an extract from the piece. Say the beat count silently in your head and sniff or clap in the quarter rests! Remember to tap the treble-clef rhythms with your right hand and the bass-clef rhythms with your left hand.

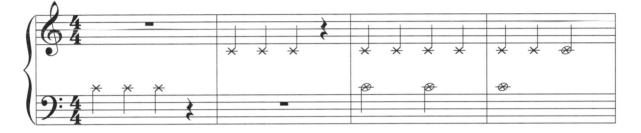

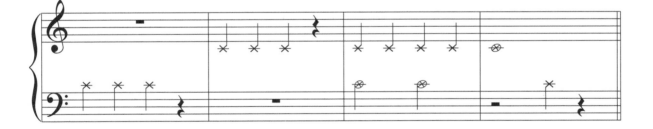

NOTE FOCUS

During the first four measures of this piece, you will be clapping and "knocking!" Clap the notes that appear in the treble clef (right-hand part) and gently knock your left-hand knuckles on the piano lid for the notes in the bass clef (left-hand part). You'll also have to knock on the piano lid for the very final measure!

IN THE SPOTLIGHT

SOLO

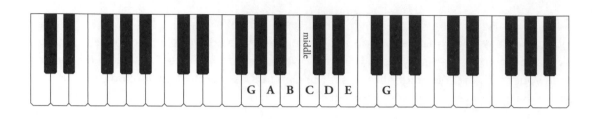

Bright and Cheerful

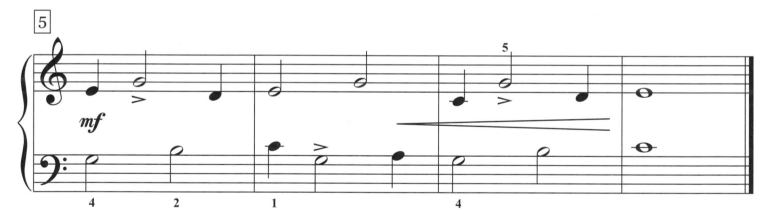

PERFORMANCE NOTES

If you are in the spotlight it means you are the focus of attention, like an actor on a stage. Below, you can find out who the star of this piece is!

RHYTHM FOCUS

When a piece of music has four beats per bar, the most important (or strong) beats are 1 and 3. However, "In the Spotlight" has accent marks on beat 2, meaning we should play the notes on this beat with a heavier touch. Making beat 2 more important than beat 1 creates an effect known as *syncopation*. Beat 2 is really in the spotlight here!

Practice this syncopation using the following exercise. Clap the rhythm but make sure you clap more loudly on beat-count 2. Say the beat count, making "2" louder than the other numbers.

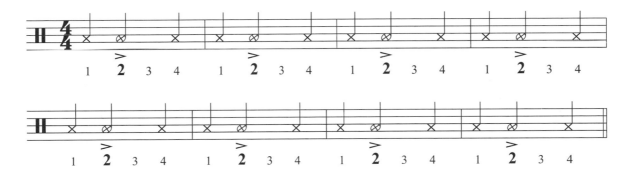

When you practice the music, remember to give every half note two full beats!

NOTE FOCUS

Your hands play together from measures 4–8. This might need slow, steady practice to make sure the notes in each hand are played at exactly the right moment. Aim to count a steady four beats per bar.

ON THE TIGHTROPE

SOLO

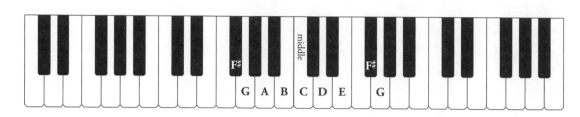

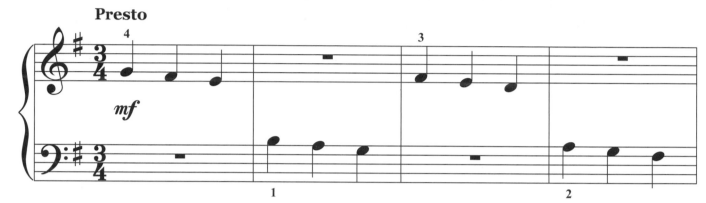

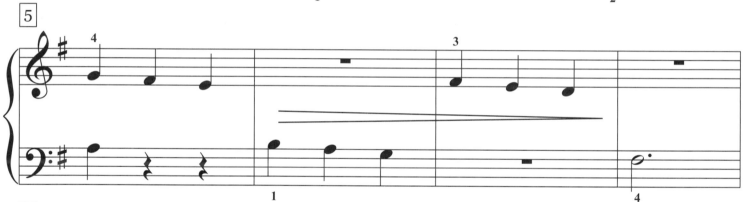

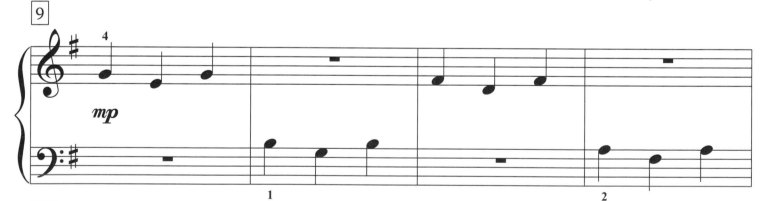

PERFORMANCE NOTES

There's always a risk, when walking a tightrope, that you might fall off! "Presto" means to play fast, so make sure you know the notes really well and hold on tight!

RHYTHM FOCUS

Let's play tic-tac-toe! Ask your teacher to play with you using quarter notes (the 0s), and you can play using dotted half notes (the Xs). Place the dotted half notes in a row of three before your teacher places their quarter notes and you have won the game! To help, a dotted half note has already been added.

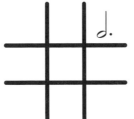

NOTE FOCUS

Non-legato is a useful touch to learn; it's somewhere between playing very smooth and very short notes. The hands are mostly playing separately during this piece, so that you can focus on working on your non-legato touch. Keep the fingers close to the keys, but be sure to take your finger completely off before moving on to the next note. This should produce a very short "gap" in the sound between every note. You can practice your non-legato touch with the following exercise, alternating each measure with very short notes. Repeat the exercise using different fingers.

The sharp sign (♯) written at the beginning of the score is part of the *key signature*. Here, it means that every time you read an F on the music be sure to play an F♯ instead (the black note to the right of the white F key).

Can you find all the F♯s on your piano? It's fun to play each one firmly with the second finger of the right hand, moving up and down the keyboard.

A LITTLE BIT SAD

SOLO WITH TEACHER ACCOMPANIMENT

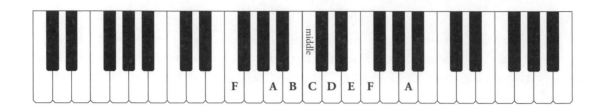

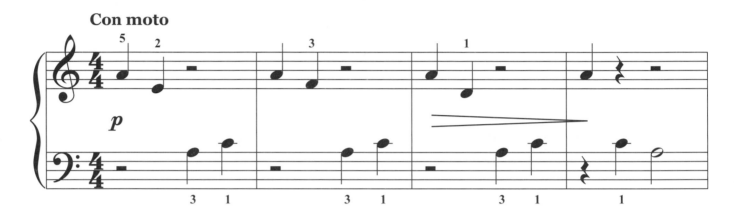

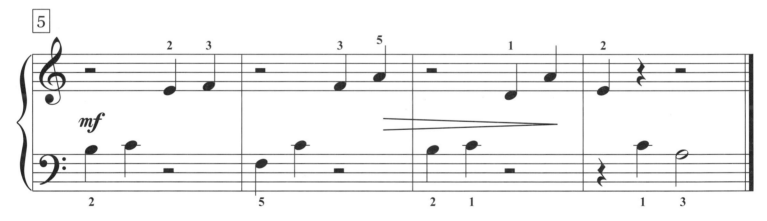

PERFORMANCE NOTES

This piece has a sad mood, in part created by the fact that it is in a minor key (A minor). But avoid playing it too slowly; you should strive to keep the music flowing!

RHYTHM FOCUS

To tap the rhythm of "A Little Bit Sad," you'll need both hands. Be sure to use the right hand to tap the note values in the treble clef and the left hand for those in the bass clef. Say the beat count as you tap ("1, 2, 3, 4").

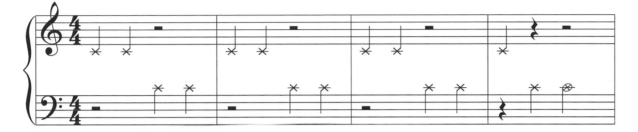

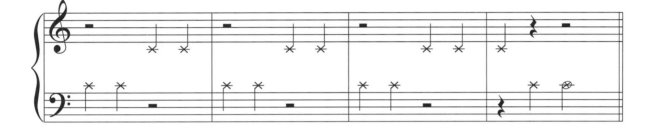

NOTE FOCUS

If you play the piece as a solo without the teacher accompaniment and you are able to play the pedals, you could try keeping the right (sustaining) pedal depressed for the whole piece. This will result in a wonderful "echo" effect.

Use your best *legato* or smooth finger touch by joining every note carefully. Practice playing as quietly as you can at the end.

SNAP

SOLO

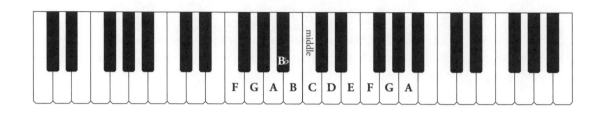

Softly and Steadily

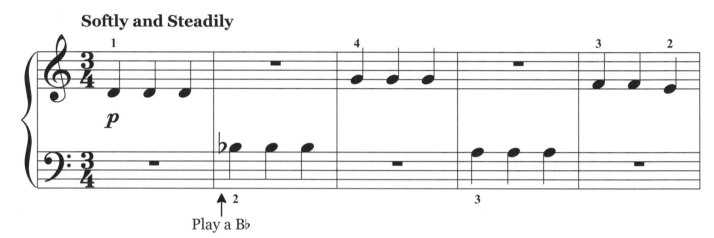

Play a B♭

PERFORMANCE NOTES

Snap is a popular card game. Players deal cards and react quickly to spot pairs of cards with the same picture. When they see two identical cards, they say, "snap." In this piece, the right and left hand are also playing a similar game.

RHYTHM FOCUS

Plenty of quarter notes feature in this piece. Tap the rhythm with both hands on your piano lid. Then, ask your teacher to clap the left-hand part while you clap the right-hand part. Now, you clap the left-hand part and your teacher claps the right-hand part. Be sure to keep the pulse absolutely steady and try not to miss a beat!

NOTE FOCUS

Play the quarter notes with a *non-legato* touch, taking your finger off each key just after it has been depressed and creating a crisp, elegant sound. Notes often repeat or appear several times in this piece. Aim to play repeated notes with the same amount of *tone* (or sound) and be sure to play the B♭ firmly.

How softly can you play the repeated notes? Practice depressing each key very slowly. The slower you press down the key, the softer the sound will be. The quicker you play or press down the key, the louder the note. Try this exercise, changing your tone color on every note.

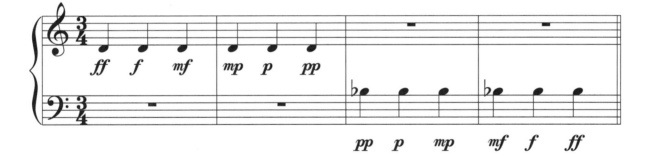

41

COTTON CANDY

DUET

PERFORMANCE NOTES

This duet offers the opportunity to play with a fellow piano student. Perhaps you can give a performance to your friends, family, or school class? Playing music with friends is so special. "Cotton Candy" is a wonderfully sweet piano duet, a fluffy and delicious treat just like the sugary candy, which is usually served on a stick.

RHYTHM FOCUS

Practice playing together by tapping the rhythm of the two parts on your piano lid at the same time. To warm up, try tapping the following simple rhythm also with your duet partner. You can tap the exercise at different speeds to really test yourselves!

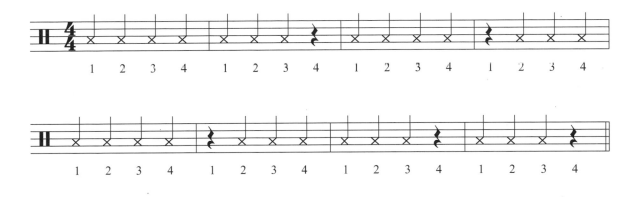

NOTE FOCUS

In this piece, the "Player 1" part needs to be played an octave higher than written to avoid the bumping of hands. This is indicated in the music with the following symbol: 8va - - - - - - - -

The melody is passed between both parts; make sure you are both aware of who is playing the tune at any moment. You should play the melody with a full tone, while keeping the other notes soft.

CHILI-PEPPER RAG

SOLO

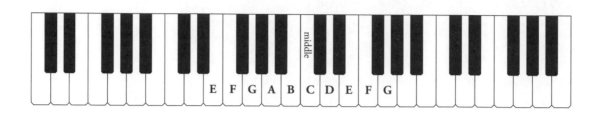

Fast & Rhythmical

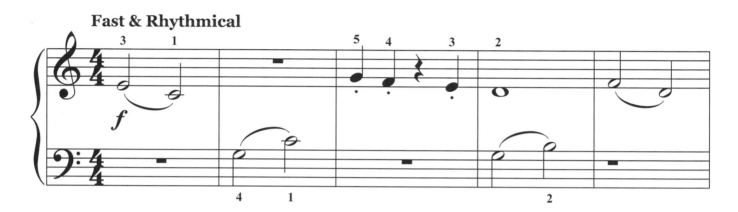

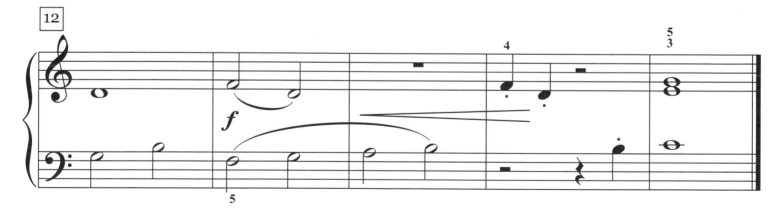

PERFORMANCE NOTES

Chili peppers are hot. And this piece calls for a fast tempo, as if you are running for a glass of water after eating hot chilis! A piano rag comes from a genre called ragtime, which was popular in North America around the beginning of the twentieth century. This music uses elements found in the ragtime style.

RHYTHM FOCUS

One of the elements of ragtime is placing a rest on the third beat. "Chili-Pepper Rag" contains lots of these third-beat rests. Draw a circle around all of them to make sure you count accurately.

You'll need to count carefully throughout, ensuring that the longer whole and half notes are held for their full value. Here's a reminder of the note values and their count.

QUARTER NOTE

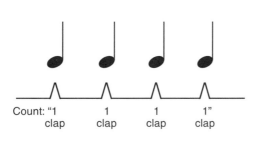

HALF NOTE

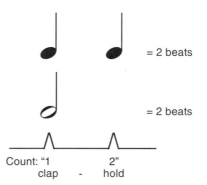

DOTTED HALF NOTE

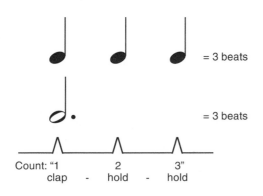

WHOLE NOTE

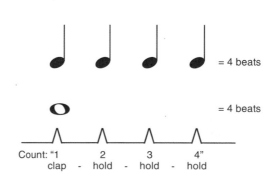

THE GRAND PALACE

PIANO SOLO

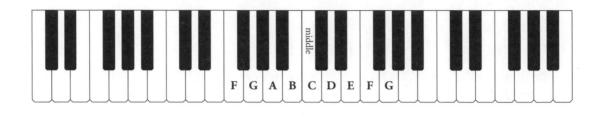

Maestoso

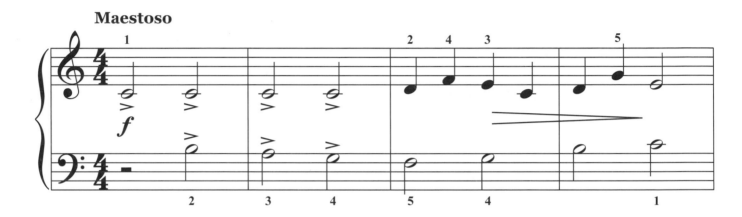

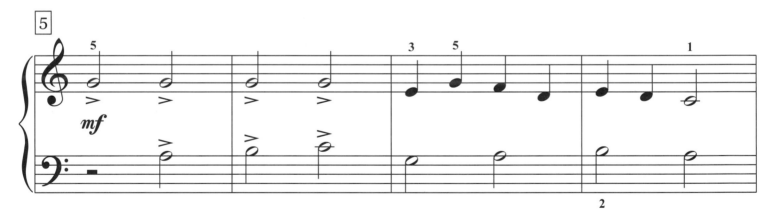

PERFORMANCE NOTES

Close your eyes and imagine a huge, beautiful palace. Who lives there? How many rooms does it have? Visualize standing outside in its amazing gardens, staring up in wonder. Keep this in mind when you are playing the music.

RHYTHM FOCUS

Try tapping the rhythm to make sure you are totally secure; practice hands separately first and then hands together. The last four measures are the trickiest, so tap them separately using the exercise below. Remember to tap the treble-clef rhythm with your right hand and the bass-clef rhythm with your left hand. If it helps, say the beat count as you tap ("1, 2, 3, 4").

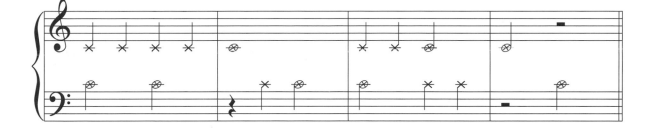

NOTE FOCUS

Your hands will play together here, so be mindful of practicing hands separately first. This will ensure that you know each musical line very well before playing them together.

The accents (>) placed above or below some noteheads tell you to play those notes with greater weight, highlighting the "grandness" of the palace.

ANGRY WASP

SOLO WITH TEACHER ACCOMPANIMENT

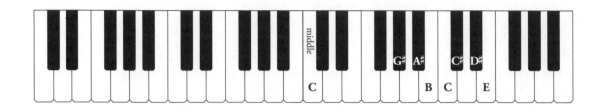

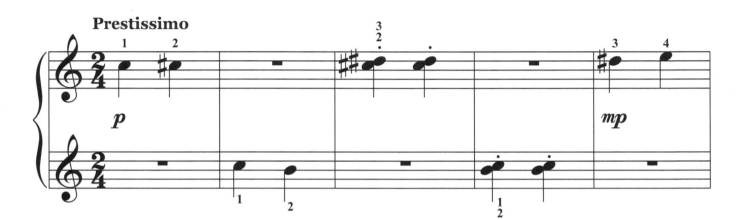

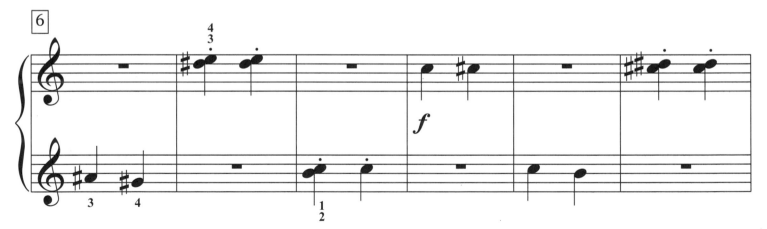

PERFORMANCE NOTES

Nobody wants to see or hear an angry wasp! This one just won't go away. It flies in from afar, becoming louder and louder.

NOTE FOCUS

The solo part consists of sharps, which help to create the angry "buzzing" of the wasp. To find the C♯ (e.g., in measure 1), locate C and play the black key immediately to its right. Check the keyboard diagram at the top of the music to help.

The suggested fingering will help you locate the notes with ease; try to keep your fingers hovering over the correct notes.

Dyads at measures 3, 4, 7, 8, 11, 12, 15, and 16 demand a very short, *staccato* sound. Aim to leave the notes as quickly as possible as if the keys are red hot. But be careful not to rush! (Keep a steady beat count.) You could practice playing these using the exercise below. Play it slowly until you are comfortable.

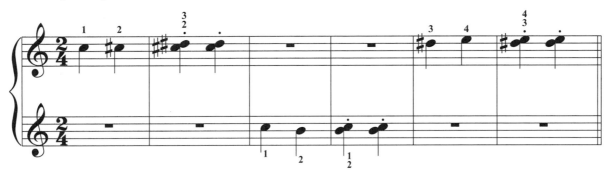

ACCOMPANIMENT

49

BALLET DANCER

SOLO

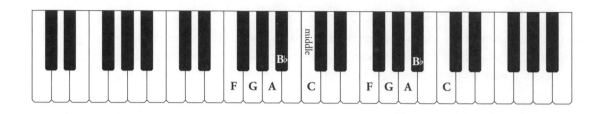

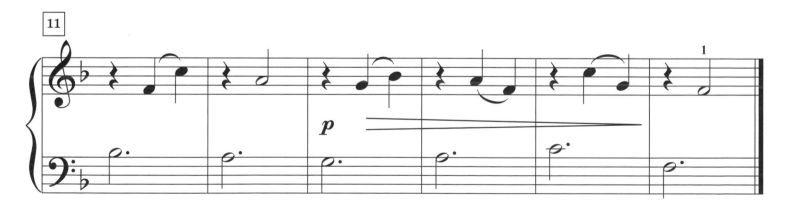

PERFORMANCE NOTES

A skilful ballet dancer takes to the stage, floating through the air with serenity and grace. Try to make your performance flowing and gentle.

RHYTHM FOCUS

Let's play tic-tac-toe! Ask your teacher to play with you using dotted half notes (the 0s), and you can play using quarter notes (the Xs). Place the quarter notes in a row of three before your teacher places their dotted half notes and you have won the game! To help, a quarter note has already been added.

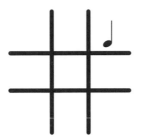

NOTE FOCUS

Hands play together throughout this piece, so try to learn each hand separately at first. The left-hand part should be smooth, each note joining to the next as though your fingers are walking along the key. The right-hand part contains the melody and will therefore need a stronger sound.

Slurred quarter notes are a feature in this piece. They are akin to a *drop-roll* movement. Drop the hand and wrist as you play the first note in each pair, connecting smoothly to the second note. Then, the hand and wrist move upwards and slightly forwards as your finger rolls off the second note.

CHEESE ON TOAST

DUET

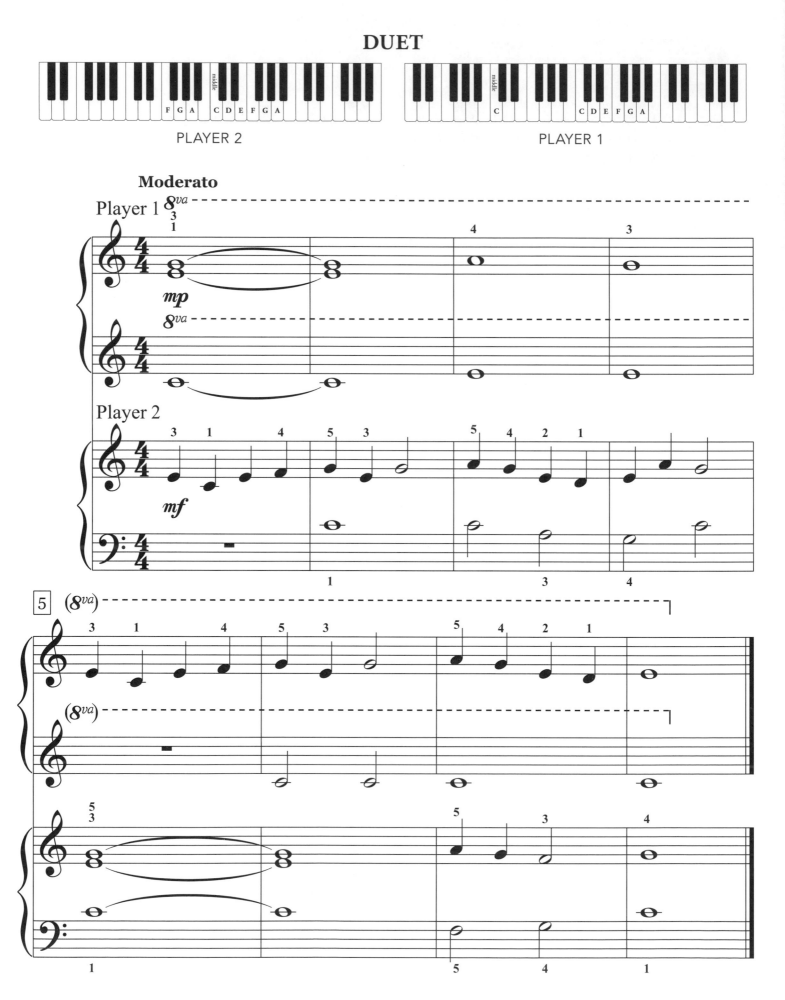

PERFORMANCE NOTES

"Cheese on Toast" offers the opportunity to play with a fellow piano student. Music is a gift that should be shared with friends, just like good food.

RHYTHM FOCUS

Practice playing together by tapping the rhythm of your parts on the piano lid, making sure you say the beat count together, too. Once you have mastered this, tap with dynamic markings. Practice this by tapping the simple rhythm below. You can try it at a number of different speeds to improve your ability to play as a duo.

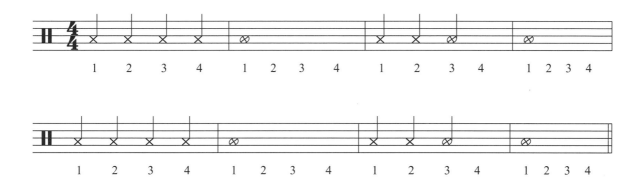

NOTE FOCUS

In this piece, the "Player 1" part needs to be played an octave higher than written, so that you are not bumping into your partner. This is indicated in the music with the following symbol:

8va - - - - - - -

Both players will need to move hand positions by just one note at measure 7 (right-hand parts). "Player 1" will also need to move at measure 5, and "Player 2" at measure 3.

Also available in the series...

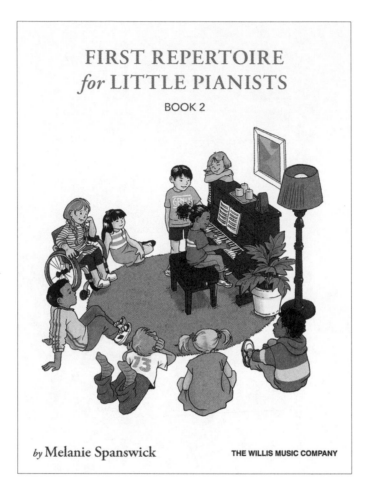

FIRST REPERTOIRE *for* LITTLE PIANISTS

BOOK 2

HL00385234

Available at all good music stores.